CW00322170

INDIAN CUISINE

Written by Harmeet Hooren-Sagoo

KUDOS

Published by Kudos, an imprint of Top That! Publishing plc.
Copyright © 2005 Top That! Publishing plc,
Tide Mill Way, Woodbridge, Suffolk, IP12 IAP.
www.topthatpublishing.com

Kudos is a Trademark of Top That! Publishing plc

Contents

4

Introduction

Indian cuisine is becoming more and more popular worldwide. The range of dishes – often just called 'curry' as a general catch-all – forms the staple diet of the Indian sub-continent.

The term 'curry' was adopted by the British Raj in the 19th century and became known in the West as the general expression for Indian cuisine. However, in Indian households curry isn't a word that is widely used, and instead the individual dishes are called by their Indian names.

The ingredients and character of the dishes vary depending on the region from which they originate.

North western India is predominantly a wheat-growing region and so Indian breads, such as chapatti (roti) and paranthas, form part of the staple diet. A curry here consists of a 'tarka' – a basic gravy used as the basis for a dish consisting of a mixture of cooked onions, garlic, ginger and spices (usually chilli, salt, turmeric and tomatoes). In the southern regions rice is grown, therefore rice dishes dominate the cuisine. Fish and seafood are also very popular.

There is a wide selection of vegetarian dishes in Indian cuisine. Indeed, the state of Gujarat, in west India, follows a strict vegetarian diet.

The spiciness of a curry depends on the amount of chilli used in the dish. Curries do not have to be hot. Removing the seeds from the chillies or adding cream or coconut milk will make a curry milder. For example a Korma is a very mild and thick sauce cooked with cream and fresh herbs. A madras curry, which originates from Madras in India is a fairly hot curry cooked in a rich sauce. The hottest curry dishes available are vindaloo or phall dishes.

The Indian sub-continent contains many different cultures and religions including Hindus, Sikhs and Muslims. This has influenced the development of Indian cuisine. For example, the cow is sacred in India and so beef curries are almost never found. The meat used is either mutton, lamb, chicken or goat.

Cow's milk, however, is used in many different ways in Indian cuisine. It is used to make yoghurts and curds such as Indian cheese - paneer (see page 9).

Milk is also used to make the popular Indian beverage, 'lassi' (see page 124). In the West, beer is the traditional accompaniment to curry and there are a number of Indian beers such as Cobra lager and Kingfisher. However in India it is lassi - a yoghurt-based drink - that is traditionally drunk with a curry.

Whether you are looking to create an authentic taste of India, or simply wishing to broaden your culinary skills, this book will give you new ideas, techniques and recipes that will really spice up your kitchen.

Basic Equipment

Heavy-based saucepan

Frying pan

Karahi (double handled 'wok'-style cooking and serving bowl)

Rolling pin

Metal slotted or perforated spoon

Clean tea towels

Wooden spoons

Weighing scales

Measuring jug

Sieve

Muslin cloths

The preparation and cooking times in these recipes are approximate and will depend upon whether you are using gas or electricity, and how familiar you are with the recipes.

Imperial weight conversions are approximate. For best results use either metric or imperial measurements throughout the recipe.

Basic Ingredients

The spices and ingredients used in this book can be bought from your local Indian grocers or may be available in the supermarket. Most of the spices used are ground spices that can be bought in packets. When using fresh green chillies in these recipes you can decide whether to deseed the chilli or not. The curry will be hotter if you leave the seeds in.

Garam Masala

Garam masala – a blend of spices – is particularly important and is used in most curries. You can buy pre-packed garam masala or mix the spices yourself as follows:

50 g (2 oz) cinnamon
50 g (2 oz) cloves
50 g (2 oz) white cumin seeds
50 g (2 oz) coriander seeds
50 g (2 oz) black cardamom seeds
50 g (2 oz) black peppercorns (optional)

Ghee (clarified butter)

Ghee is another important component of Indian cuisine. For a truly authentic taste you can use the following recipe. However, this is not absolutely essential; the more health-conscious cook can substitute olive, vegetable or sunflower oil in recipes that call for ghee.

250 g (9 oz) butter
1 tsp lemon juice
medium-sized jar

Place the butter in a saucepan on a low heat. Heat the butter until melted.

Add the lemon juice and simmer for 10 minutes.

The butter will separate and the fat will be left at the bottom. The ghee will remain on the top.

Strain the mixture in a sieve, discarding the bottom layer, and transfer the ghee to a jar to set.

Homemade yoghurt (Dahi)

This is used in Indian cuisine to cool the spiciness of a dish, and is also the chief ingredient of raita (page 108).

560 ml (20 fl oz) milk – full fat or semi-skimmed
1 tsp plain yoghurt

Boil the milk in a pan and then leave to cool. When it is lukewarm, place the milk in an insulated dish. If an insulated dish isn't available then place in a normal dish in a warm place covered tightly with a cloth.

Add the yoghurt. Leave for 5 hours or overnight to set.

Paneer – Indian cheese

This forms the basis of Mutter Paneer (page 44) and Saag Paneer (page 46).

2.3 litres (4 pts) full fat milk

2-3 tbsp white wine vinegar

muslin cloth

In a pan, boil the milk over a medium heat being careful not to burn it.

Once boiled, add the vinegar to curdle the milk. Remove from the heat.

Place a muslin cloth in a sieve or colander and strain the milk mixture. You will be left with the curds, or paneer.

Wrap up the paneer in the cloth and place a weight on top of the cloth. Leave for 15 minutes.

The paneer can then be cut into chunks or used loose - it needs to be lightly fried before use.

Chicken Tikka Masala

CHICKEN MARINADE

1 tsp grated ginger

1 tsp grated garlic

1 tsp ground coriander

1 tsp ground cumin

1 tsp chilli powder

6 tbsp natural yoghurt

1 tsp salt

2 tbsp lemon juice

1 tsp tomato purée

1 tsp turmeric

1 tsp paprika

1 tsp chicken tikka masala powder

900 g (2 lb) chicken breast (cubed)

1 medium onion, chopped

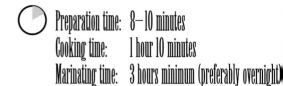

Preparation time: 8–10 minutes

Cooking time: 1 hour 10 minutes

Marinating time: 3 hours minimum (preferably overnight)

Serves: 6

For the chicken

1. Place the ginger, garlic, coriander, cumin and chilli powder in a mixing bowl and blend together.

2. Add the yoghurt, salt, lemon, tomato purée, turmeric, paprika and chicken tikka masala powder.

3. Cut the chicken into small pieces and add to the spice and yoghurt mixture. Marinate the chicken for at least 3 hours or overnight.

4. Place the chopped onions in the bottom of a baking tray or glass heatproof dish.

5. Preheat the oven to 250°C/475°F/gas mark 9 and place the marinated chicken pieces on top of the onions and cook for 40-45 minutes, turning over occasionally. While the chicken is cooking prepare the sauce. Alternatively, serve the chicken without the sauce for classic chicken tikka.

SAUCE

100 g (3 ½ oz) raw
cashew nuts

200 ml (7 fl oz) double cream

800 g (1 lb 12 oz) tinned
tomatoes, chopped

1 tbsp tomato purée

3 tsp sugar

1 tsp salt

2 tsp white cumin seeds

1 tsp chilli powder

1 tsp garam masala

1 large knob of butter

A bunch fresh coriander

For the sauce

1. Place the cashew nuts into a blender and blend
   for a few seconds. Add half the cream.

2. Place the mixture in a pan with the tinned
   tomatoes, tomato purée, sugar, salt, cumin seeds,
   chilli powder and garam masala. Simmer for 25
   minutes, adding a little water if necessary. Stir
   the mixture occasionally to prevent it from
   sticking.

3. Add the cooked chicken tikka to the sauce and
   stir in the butter, the remaining cream and the
   coriander. Taste the sauce and check the
   seasoning, adding more salt or chilli if required.

   Serve garnished with more fresh coriander
   if desired.

Chicken Korma

25 g (1 oz) flaked almonds

1 tsp ginger, grated

1 tsp garlic, grated

1 tsp white cumin seeds

1 tsp ground coriander

1 tsp paprika

½ tsp chilli powder

4 tbsp natural yoghurt

4 chicken breasts

3 tbsp oil

1 medium onion,
finely chopped

½ tsp salt

1 tbsp lemon juice

200 ml (7 fl oz) water

150 ml (5 fl oz) double cream

1 tsp sugar

2 tbsp coconut milk

handful fresh coriander,
chopped

1 tsp garam masala

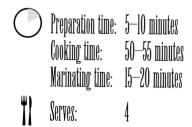

Preparation time: 5–10 minutes
Cooking time: 50–55 minutes
Marinating time: 15–20 minutes

Serves: 4

Directions

1. Roast the almonds on a baking tray in a hot oven for a few minutes. Mix the ginger, garlic, white cumin seeds, ground coriander, paprika, chilli powder with the almonds and the yoghurt.

2. Marinate chicken in the yoghurt and spice mixture for 15-20 minutes.

3. Heat the oil in a pan. Add the onion and cook until golden brown.

4. Add the marinated chicken pieces, the salt and lemon juice and cook for 5-7 minutes.

5. Add the water, cover and simmer for 10 minutes, stirring occasionally, before adding the cream.

6. Simmer for another 10 minutes then add the sugar, coconut milk, fresh coriander and garam masala and cook for a further 3-4 minutes, stirring occasionally.

7. Serve with boiled rice and garnish with more flaked almonds.

13

Chicken Vindaloo

1 tsp ground coriander
1 tsp white cumin seeds
4 whole cloves
5 cm (2 in.) cinnamon stick
2 tsp black peppercorns
1 tsp ground fenugreek
60 ml (2 fl oz) white vinegar
1 kg (2 lb 3 oz) chicken (boneless)
3 tbsp ghee/oil
6 garlic cloves, finely chopped
1 large onion chopped
2 tsp ginger, finely grated
3 tsp tomato paste
1 tsp salt
6 dried red or green chillies
½ tsp chilli powder
2 curry leaves
425 ml (15 fl oz) water
2 tbsp yoghurt
½- 1 tsp tandoori powder
fresh coriander

Preparation time: 5–10 minutes
Cooking time: 30–40 minutes
Marinating time: 5–8 minutes
Serves: 4–6

Directions

1. Grind all the spices in a pestle and mortar and dry fry in a pan on a medium heat for 30 seconds, then mix with the vinegar.

2. Cut the chicken into cubes and coat with the spice mixture. Leave to saturate for 5-8 minutes.

3. Heat the ghee/oil in a saucepan and sauté the meat until it is evenly coloured.

4. Finely chop the garlic, onion and ginger and add to the pan. Cook for 5-8 minutes until the onions are soft, then add the tomato paste, salt, dried chillies and chilli powder. Cook for 2-3 minutes

5. Add the curry leaves and water, cover and cook on a moderate heat for 15-20 minutes, stirring occasionally. Then remove the lid, add the yoghurt and tandoori powder and cook for a further 2-3 minutes, until the sauce thickens slightly.

6. Garnish with fresh coriander leaves if desired.

14

15

Tandoori Chicken

8 chicken drumsticks or
400 g (14 oz) chicken pieces

4 tbsp yoghurt

1 ½ tsp fresh garlic, crushed

1 ½ tsp fresh ginger, grated

1 ½ tsp chilli powder

1 tsp ground cumin

1 tsp ground coriander

1 tbsp lemon juice

½ tsp salt

1 tbsp tandoori powder

Garnish with: lettuce leaves,
onions, sliced tomatoes
and lemon wedges

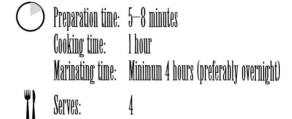

Preparation time: 5–8 minutes

Cooking time: 1 hour

Marinating time: Minimum 4 hours (preferably overnight)

Serves: 4

Directions

1. Make 2-3 slashes in each chicken drumstick so they can absorb the spices.

2. Place the yoghurt, garlic, ginger, chilli powder, ground cumin, ground coriander, lemon juice, salt and tandoori powder in a bowl and mix together.

3. Add the chicken to the mixture and stir in thoroughly. Leave to marinate in the fridge for a minimum of 4 hours, or overnight.

4. Preheat the oven to 370°F/190°C/gas mark 6. Place the chicken in a heatproof dish. Cook for 45-55 minutes turning the chicken pieces occasionally to prevent them burning.

5. Serve on a bed of lettuce and garnish with onion rings, sliced tomatoes and lemon wedges.

17

Chicken Wings

1 tbsp oil (olive, vegetable or sunflower)

1 tsp white cumin seeds

1 ½ tsp fresh ginger, grated

1 ½ tsp fresh garlic, crushed

600 g (20 oz) chicken wings

1 tsp salt

½ tsp turmeric

1 tsp chilli powder

1 tsp sun-dried tomato paste (optional)

100 g (3 ½ oz) tinned tomatoes

150 ml (5 fl oz) water

1 tsp garam masala

2 tbsp yoghurt

1 tbsp lemon juice

fresh coriander to garnish (optional)

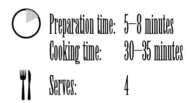

Preparation time: 5–8 minutes
Cooking time: 30–35 minutes

Serves: 4

Directions

1. Heal the oil in a kahari or heavy-based pan. Grind the cumin seeds in a pestle and mortar and stir-fry for 30 seconds. Add the ginger and garlic. Stir-fry for 1-2 minutes then add chicken wings, salt, turmeric and chilli powder.

2. Cook for 5 minutes, stirring all the time, then add the tomato paste and tinned tomatoes and water. Simmer for a further 15-20 minutes on medium heat or until the water has been absorbed.

3. Add the garam masala, yoghurt and lemon juice near the end of cooking and heat for a further minute.

4. Garnish with coriander and serve with a side salad.

18

Lamb Curry

2-3 tbsp ghee/oil

1 medium onion, chopped

1 tsp fresh garlic, grated

1 tsp fresh ginger, grated

500 g (17 ½ oz) lamb pieces

1 tsp turmeric

1 tsp salt

1 tsp chilli powder

1 tsp white cumin seeds

150 g (5 oz) tinned tomatoes

2 tbsp natural yoghurt

2 tbsp lemon juice

1 tsp meat masala (optional)

600 ml (20 fl oz) water

1 tsp garam masala

handful of fresh coriander, chopped

Note

Meat masala is a spice mixture that can be purchased as a pre-prepared mix.

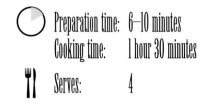

Preparation time: 6–10 minutes
Cooking time: 1 hour 30 minutes

Serves: 4

Directions

1. Heat the ghee/oil in a pan. Sauté the onions, garlic and ginger and stir-fry for 2-3 minutes. Add the lamb pieces, cover and cook for 10-15 minutes on a moderate/low heat, stirring occasionally.

2. Remove the lid and cook for a further ten minutes.

3. Add turmeric, salt, chilli powder, cumin and tomatoes and cook for 2-3 minutes. Add the yoghurt, lemon juice and meat masala (if using). Cook for 25-35 minutes on a moderate heat until the lamb is tender. Stir occasionally.

4. Add the water and cook for a further 30-40 minutes on a low heat until the liquid has halved and you are left with a thicker sauce. Finally add the garam masala and fresh coriander and cook for a final two minutes.

Minced Lamb Keema

2 tbsp oil
1 medium onion, chopped
1 tsp garlic, finely grated
1 tsp fresh ginger, grated
1 tsp turmeric
1 tsp salt
2-3 fresh green chillies, chopped
150 g (5 oz) tinned tomatoes
600 g (1 lb 5 oz) lamb mince
1 tbsp Worcestershire sauce
150 g (5 oz) peas (optional)
1 tsp garam masala
fresh coriander to garnish

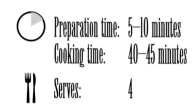

Preparation time: 5–10 minutes
Cooking time: 40–45 minutes

Serves: 4

Directions

1. Heat the oil in a medium-sized pan. Sauté the finely chopped onions until golden brown, stirring occasionally. Add garlic and ginger and stir-fry for a further 2-3 minutes.

2. Add the turmeric, salt, fresh chillies and tomatoes and cook for 2-3 minutes.

3. Add the minced lamb and Worcestershire sauce to the pan and mix together with the spice mixture. Cook for 30-40 minutes on a medium heat, stirring occasionally.

4. Add the peas, if using, and the garam masala and cook for a further five minutes.

5. Serve garnished with fresh coriander.

Lamb In Spinach

600 g (1 lb 5 oz) lean lamb

2 tbsp of ghee/oil

2 medium onions chopped

1 tsp fresh ginger, finely grated

1 tsp fresh garlic, grated

100 g (3 ½ oz) tomatoes

1 green chilli, chopped

½ tsp of turmeric

1 tsp salt

1 kg (2 lb 3 oz) tinned, frozen or fresh, trimmed and washed spinach

300 ml (10 ½ fl oz) water

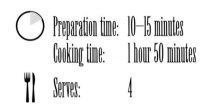

Preparation time: 10—15 minutes

Cooking time: 1 hour 50 minutes

Serves: 4

Directions

1. Trim the lamb and cut into bite-size pieces. Heat the ghee/oil in a medium-sized pan.

2. Sauté the onions, ginger and garlic for 2-3 minutes, then add the lamb pieces. Cover and cook for ten minutes on a low heat, stirring occasionally. Remove the lid and cook for a further ten minutes.

3. Add the tomatoes, chilli, turmeric and salt to the mixture and stir-fry for 3-4 minutes.

4. Add 200 ml of the water, cover and cook for 35-40 minutes.

5. Add the spinach and the rest of the water and cook for a further 45-55 minutes on a low heat. If the lamb is not tender then increase the heat slightly and cook uncovered until the surplus liquid has been absorbed, then cook for a further 8-10 minutes.

6. Serve with rice or naan (page 89).

25

Lamb Chops

1 tbsp oil
1 medium onion, finely chopped
1 ½ tsp garlic, finely grated
1 ½ tsp fresh ginger,
finely grated
100 g (3 ½ oz) tinned tomatoes
½ tsp turmeric
1 tsp salt
1-2 fresh green chillies, chopped
450 g (1 lb) lamb chops
1 tbsp lemon juice
200 ml (7 fl oz) water
1 tsp garam masala
fresh coriander to garnish

Preparation time: 10–12 minutes
Cooking time: 1 hour 15 minutes

Serves: 4

Directions

1. Heat the oil and fry the onions until golden brown. Add the garlic and ginger and stir-fry for two minutes. Add the tomatoes, turmeric, salt and chillies. Fry for 3-5 minutes.

2. Place the lamb in the spice mixture and cook for 5-10 minutes. Add the lemon juice and water and cook for an hour on a low heat, stirring occasionally.

3. Near the end of cooking add the garam masala. Garnish with fresh coriander.

27

Lamb Kebabs

450 g (1 lb) minced lamb

breadcrumbs from one slice of bread

1 tsp garlic, finely grated

1 tsp garam masala

1 tsp ginger, finely grated

2 fresh green chillies, chopped

1 medium onion, finely chopped

1 tbsp soy sauce

$\frac{1}{2}$ tsp turmeric

1 tbsp of lemon juice

$\frac{1}{2}$ bunch fresh coriander, freshly chopped

Preparation time: 10 minutes

Cooking time: 15–20 minutes

Serves: 4

Directions

1. Place all the ingredients in a large mixing bowl. Mix together and knead into a ball.
2. Divide the mixture into eight patties or eight kebab shapes.
3. Cook under a grill on a medium heat for 8-10 minutes until each side has browned. Turn over halfway through cooking. Alternatively, cook over a hot barbeque on skewers.
4. Serve with a side salad.

Tip

You can use half an egg to help bind the mixture rather than breadcrumbs if you prefer.

Lamb Meatballs

450 g (1 lb) lean lamb mince
½ a raw egg
1 tsp garam masala
1 tsp salt
2 tbsp ghee/olive oil
1 medium onion, finely chopped
1 ½ tsp ground coriander
1 ½ tsp garlic, finely grated
1 ½ tsp ginger, finely grated
1 fresh green chilli, chopped
½ tsp ground cumin
150 g (5 oz) tinned tomatoes
½ tsp turmeric
1 tsp soy sauce
350 g (12 fl oz) water
fresh coriander or chillies
to garnish

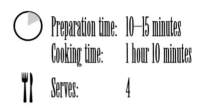

Preparation time: 10–15 minutes
Cooking time: 1 hour 10 minutes

Serves: 4

Directions

1. Mix together the lamb mince, egg, garam masala and salt in a mixing bowl. Shape the mixture into 16 balls.

2. Heat the ghee/oil in a saucepan and sauté the onion, ground coriander, garlic, ginger, chilli and cumin for 5 minutes, stirring occasionally. Add the tomatoes, turmeric and soy sauce, and cook for 3-4 minutes.

3. Add the meatballs to the saucepan and cook, covered, for 15-20 minutes on a low heat and stir gently.

4. Add the water and cook for a further 30-40 minutes on a low heat.

5. Garnish with fresh coriander if desired and serve on a bed of rice.

Fish Pakora

550 g (1 lb 3 oz) cod fillets
1 tbsp lemon juice
200 g (7 oz) gram flour
½ bunch of fresh coriander, chopped
1 fresh green chilli, chopped
1 tsp salt
½ tsp turmeric
200 ml (7 fl oz) water
450 ml (16 fl oz) oil
lemon wedges
lettuce leaves

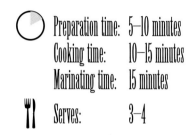

Preparation time: 5–10 minutes
Cooking time: 10–15 minutes
Marinating time: 15 minutes

Serves: 3–4

Directions

1. Cut the cod fillets into bite size pieces and marinate with the lemon juice for a few minutes.

2. Place the gram flour, fresh coriander, chilli, salt and turmeric in a mixing bowl and mix together.

3. Add the water to the gram flour mixture until the mixture is of the consistency of a batter. Coat the marinated fish pieces in the batter. Leave to marinate for 15 minutes.

4. Place the oil in a pan to deep fry the fish (oil should be on a medium heat). Fry the fish until golden brown – approximately five minutes.

5. Once the fish is cooked, lift out of the oil with a perforated metal spoon and pat off any excess oil with kitchen towel.

6. Serve the pakoras on a bed of lettuce with lemon wedges.

33

Fish Curry

1 tsp mustard seeds
1 tsp white cumin seeds
3-4 tbsp oil
550 g (1 lb 3 oz) skinless
cod fillets
1 medium onion, finely sliced
1 ½ tsp ginger, finely grated
1 ½ tsp of fresh garlic,
finely grated
150 g (5 oz) tinned tomatoes
1 fresh tomato, diced
1 tsp salt
1 tsp chilli powder
½ tsp turmeric
200 ml (7 fl oz) coconut milk
fresh coriander, to garnish

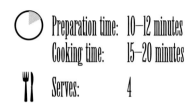

Preparation time: 10–12 minutes
Cooking time: 15–20 minutes

Serves: 4

Directions

1. Grind the mustard seeds and white cumin seeds in a pestle and mortar.

2. Heat half the oil in a large frying pan and cook the fish for one minute each side, so it is sealed.

3. Heat the remaining oil in a kahari or large heavy-based pan and add the mustard seeds and white cumin seeds. Stir-fry for 30 seconds. Add the onion and sauté on a medium heat until golden brown.

4. Add the ginger, garlic and stir-fry for three minutes. Add the tinned tomatoes and fresh tomato, salt, chilli powder, turmeric and the fish and cook for a further 3-5 minutes. Add the coconut milk and cook for a further 2-5 minutes.

5. Garnish with fresh coriander and serve.

Baked Fish

4 cod or white fish fillets

4 tbsp olive oil or ghee

2 curry leaves

2 small onions, finely chopped

1 ½ tsp garlic, finely grated

1 ½ tsp ginger, finely grated

4 large fresh tomatoes

1 tsp ground cumin

½ tsp turmeric

1 tsp salt

1 tsp mango powder

1 tsp fenugreek seeds

2 tsp chilli powder

½ tsp black peppercorns

3 tbsp double cream

fresh basil or coriander to garnish (optional)

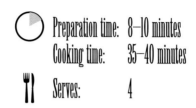

Preparation time: 8–10 minutes
Cooking time: 35–40 minutes

Serves: 4

Directions

1. Clean and rinse the fish fillet under cold water. Drain and wipe dry. Make deep cuts in the flesh to allow the spices to penetrate the fish. Set aside.

2. Heat half the oil and stir-fry the curry leaves for 30 seconds, then seal the fish for 30 seconds on each side. Remove the fish and place in an ovenproof dish.

3. Heat the remaining oil in a fresh karahi and add the chopped onions, garlic and ginger and cook for ten minutes until the onions are golden brown.

4. Dice the tomatoes and add to the pan with the cumin, turmeric, salt, mango powder, fenugreek, chilli powder and peppercorns. Cook for 3-4 minutes. Remove the pan from the heat and stir in the cream.

5. Pre-heat the oven to 350°F/180°C/gas mark 4. Place the fish fillets in a baking dish, pour the sauce over the top and bake for 20 minutes.

6. Garnish with fresh basil or coriander if desired.

37

Prawn Curry

1 tsp white cumin seeds
2 tbsp oil
2 bay leaves
1 small onion, finely chopped
1 tsp garlic, finely grated
1 tsp ginger, finely grated
½ tsp turmeric
1 fresh green chilli, chopped
1 tsp salt
½ tsp black peppercorns
100 g (3 ½ oz) tinned tomatoes
250 g (9 oz) raw king prawns
½ tsp garam masala
150 ml (5 fl oz) double cream

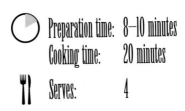

Preparation time: 8–10 minutes
Cooking time: 20 minutes
Serves: 4

Directions

1. Grind the white cumin seeds in a pestle and mortar. Heat the oil in a saucepan and stir-fry the white cumin seeds and bay leaves for a few seconds.

2. Add the chopped onion, garlic and ginger and sauté until the onions are golden brown.

3. Add the turmeric, fresh chilli, salt, black peppercorns and tinned tomatoes and cook for five minutes.

4. Stir the prawns and garam masala into the mixture and cook for 3-4 minutes. Take the pan off the heat to stir in the cream and then return to the heat and cook for a further 2-3 minutes. Leave the dish to stand for 1-2 minutes before serving. Serve on a bed of rice.

38

Tandoori Prawns

3 tbsp yoghurt

1 ½ tsp fresh garlic, crushed

1 ½ tsp fresh ginger, grated

1 ½ tsp chilli powder

1 tsp ground cumin

1 tsp ground coriander

1 tbsp lemon juice

½ tsp salt

1 tbsp tandoori powder

250 g (9 oz) king prawns

½ tbsp oil

garnish with: lettuce leaves, sliced onions, sliced tomatoes and lemon wedges

Preparation time: 5 minutes

Cooking time: 5–8 minutes

Marinating time: 20 mins

Serves: 4

Directions

1. Place the yoghurt, garlic, ginger, chilli powder, ground cumin, ground coriander, lemon juice, salt and tandoori powder in a bowl and mix together.

2. Add the prawns to the mixture and marinate well. Leave to marinate in the fridge for 20 minutes.

3. Heat the oil in a heavy-based saucepan. Cook the prawn mixture over a medium heat for 2-3 minutes. Transfer to a grill pan and cook under a hot grill for 1-2 minutes, until crisp.

Mixed Vegetable Curry

3 tbsp ghee/oil
1 tsp black mustard seeds
1 tsp white cumin seeds
3 or 4 curry leaves
1 medium sized onion, chopped
1 tsp garlic, finely grated
1 tsp ginger, finely grated
1 fresh tomato
100 g (3 ½ oz) tinned tomatoes
1 tsp chilli powder
½ tsp turmeric
1 tsp salt
2 medium potatoes, diced
½ medium cauliflower, diced
200 g (7 oz) frozen or
fresh peas
200 g (7 oz) frozen
mixed vegetables
300 ml (10 ½ fl oz) water
1 tbsp lemon juice
1 tsp garam masala
fresh coriander to garnish
(optional)

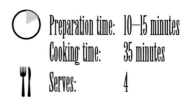

Preparation time: 10–15 minutes
Cooking time: 35 minutes
Serves: 4

Directions

1. Heat the ghee/oil in a saucepan. Grind the mustard and cumin seeds in a pestle and mortar then add to the pan. Add curry leaves and stir-fry for ten seconds until they turn a shade darker.

2. Add the onion, garlic and ginger and sauté gently until the onions are golden brown.

3. Add the fresh and tinned tomatoes, chilli powder, turmeric and salt and stir well. Cook for three minutes.

4. Add the potatoes, cauliflower, peas and frozen mixed vegetables and stir-fry for five minutes.

5. Add the water, cover and leave to simmer on a medium heat for 10-12 minutes, stirring occasionally. The vegetables should be tender. If they are not, cook for a further 3-4 minutes, adding more water if necessary.

6. Add the lemon juice and garam masala to the pan. Cover and leave to simmer for a further 2-3 minutes, stirring occasionally.

7. Turn off the heat once the vegetables are cooked and leave for 2-3 minutes before serving. Transfer to a plate and garnish with fresh coriander.

43

Peas & Cheese (Mutter Paneer)

6 tbsp ghee/oil

300 g (10 ½ oz) paneer
(see recipe on page 9)

1 medium onion, finely chopped

1 tsp garlic, grated

1 tsp ginger, grated

100 g (3 ½ oz) tinned tomatoes

½ tsp turmeric

1 tsp salt

1 fresh green chilli, chopped

½ tsp chilli powder

400 g (14 oz) peas

300 ml (10 ½ fl oz) water

1 tsp garam masala

fresh coriander (optional)

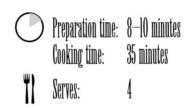

Preparation time: 8–10 minutes
Cooking time: 35 minutes

Serves: 4

Directions

1. Heat four tablespoons of the ghee/oil in a frying pan and fry the paneer pieces until golden brown on all sides.

2. Heat the remaining ghee/oil in a separate saucepan. Sauté the onion, garlic and ginger until the onions are golden brown.

3. Add the tomatoes, turmeric, salt, fresh chilli and chilli powder and stir-fry for a further two minutes.

4. Add the peas and water and simmer for 10-12 minutes.

5. Add the paneer and garam masala, and simmer for a further 3-4 minutes. Garnish with a sprig of fresh coriander.

Spinach & Cheese (Palak/Saag Paneer)

4 tbsp cooking oil

300 g (10 ½ oz) paneer
(see recipe page 9)

2 tbsp ghee/oil

2 medium onions,
finely chopped

1 tsp garlic, finely grated

1 tsp ginger, finely grated

2 fresh green chillies, chopped

1 tsp tomato purée

1 tsp salt

500 g (17 ½ oz) tinned,
frozen, or trimmed,
washed, fresh spinach

1 tsp garam masala

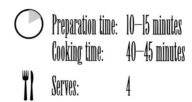

Preparation time: 10–15 minutes

Cooking time: 40–45 minutes

Serves: 4

Directions

1. Heat the oil in a frying pan and stir-fry the paneer on all sides until golden brown.

2. Heat the ghee/oil in a saucepan. Sauté the onions, garlic and ginger until the onions are golden brown.

3. Add the chillies, tomato purée and salt and stir-fry for 3-5 minutes.

4. Add the spinach and cook, stirring occasionally, for 20-25 minutes.

5. Add the garam masala and cook for a further 3-4 minutes.

6. Add the cooked paneer to the pan and stir the mixture for 2-3 minutes.

7. Serve with hot pooris (page 90), roti (page 93), or plain rice.

46

Okra Curry (Bindia – Ladies' Fingers)

450 g (1 lb) okra (ladies' fingers)
2 tbsp oil
2 medium onions, sliced
1 tsp chilli powder or
1 fresh green chilli, chopped
1 tsp salt
1/2 tsp turmeric
1 tbsp lemon juice
1/2 tsp garam masala
fresh coriander to garnish
(optional)

Preparation time: 5–10 minutes
Cooking time: 20–25 minutes

Serves: 4

Directions

1. Rinse, drain and pat the okra dry. Use a sharp knife to remove the ends and cut into 2.5 cm (1 in.) pieces.
2. Heat the oil in a large frying pan. Sauté the onions for 2 minutes.
3. Add the chilli powder, salt and turmeric and cook for one minute. Add the okra and cook on a low heat, stirring occasionally, for 10-15 minutes until the okra is tender.
4. Drizzle the lemon juice and garam masala over the mixture and leave to simmer for one minute. Garnish with coriander if desired.

49

Spinach & Potatoes (Saag Aloo)

2 tbsp ghee/oil
1 medium onion, finely chopped
1 tsp garlic, finely grated
1 tsp ginger, finely grated
1 fresh green chilli, chopped
½ tsp turmeric
1 tsp tomato purée
1 tsp salt
2 tbsp water
400 g (14 oz) tinned,
frozen, or trimmed,
washed, fresh spinach
400 g (14 oz) potatoes,
pealed and diced
½ tsp garam masala

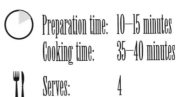

Preparation time: 10–15 minutes
Cooking time: 35–40 minutes

Serves: 4

Directions

1. Heat the ghee/oil in a saucepan. Sauté the onions, garlic and ginger until the onions are golden brown.
2. Add the chilli, turmeric, tomato purée, salt and water and stir-fry for 3-5 minutes.
3. Add the spinach and potatoes and cook, stirring occasionally, for 15-20 minutes on a medium-low heat. The potatoes should be soft and tender. If not, add a little more water and cook for a further few minutes.
4. Stir in the garam masala and cook for a further 3-4 minutes.

51

Pumpkin Curry

2-3 tbsp ghee/oil
1 tsp white cumin seeds
1 large onion, finely chopped
1 tsp mango powder
1 tsp fresh ginger, grated
1 tsp fresh garlic, grated
1 tsp chilli powder
1 tbsp tomato purée
2 tbsp lemon juice
$\frac{1}{2}$ tsp turmeric
1 tsp sugar
1 tsp salt
450 g (1 lb) orange or green pumpkin, cubed
200 ml (7 fl oz) water
200 ml (7 fl oz) double cream
$\frac{1}{2}$ tsp garam masala

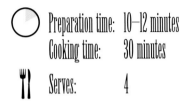

Preparation time: 10—12 minutes
Cooking time: 30 minutes

Serves: 4

Directions

1. Heat the ghee/oil in a large frying pan. Grind the cumin seeds in a pestle and mortar, then stir-fry for 30 seconds. Add the onion and cook until golden brown.

2. Add the mango powder, ginger, garlic, chilli powder, tomato purée, lemon juice, turmeric, sugar and salt to the pan and mix together. Stir-fry for 2-3 minutes.

3. Add the cubed pumpkin and stir-fry for 4-5 minutes on a medium-low heat.

4. Add the water, cover and cook over a low heat for 10-15 minutes, stirring occasionally until the pumpkin is tender.

5. Add the cream and garam masala and simmer until the pumpkin is soft. Serve with gram flour bread (page 94) or chapati/roti (page 93).

Bombay Potatoes

500 g (17 ½ oz) potatoes
2 tbsp ghee/oil
1 tsp cumin seeds
1 tsp black mustard seeds
1 tsp garlic, finely grated
1 tsp fresh ginger, grated
2 fresh green chillies, chopped
½ tsp turmeric
1 tsp salt
100 g (3 ½ oz) tinned
tomatoes or 3
large tomatoes
150 ml (5 fl oz) water
1 tsp garam masala
fresh coriander to garnish

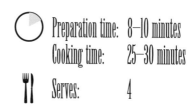

Preparation time: 8–10 minutes
Cooking time: 25–30 minutes

Serves: 4

Directions

1. Clean and rinse the potatoes and cut into cubes.
2. Heat the ghee/oil in a saucepan and stir-fry the cumin and mustard seeds on a medium heat for five seconds.
3. Add the garlic, ginger, chillies, turmeric, salt and tomatoes and stir-fry for 1-2 minutes on a medium heat.
4. Place the potatoes in the pan and coat in the mixture. Add the water and cook the potatoes for 10-15 minutes until the potatoes are tender. If the potatoes are not cooked after 15 minutes, then add another 150 ml (5 fl oz) of water and leave to simmer for a further 10 minutes.
5. Once the potatoes are cooked, add the garam masala and cook for a further 2-3 minutes.
6. Garnish with fresh coriander and serve with pooris (page 90).

Kidney Bean Curry

2 tbsp ghee/oil

1 small onion, finely chopped

1 ½ tsp garlic, finely grated

1 ½ tsp ginger, finely grated

1 tsp ground coriander

1 tsp ground cumin

2 tsp salt

2 tbsp lemon juice

½ tsp turmeric

100 g (3 ½ oz) tinned tomatoes

500 g (17 ½ oz) tinned kidney beans, drained and rinsed

1 tsp garam masala

fresh coriander to garnish (optional)

Note

You can use dried kidney beans.

Soak the beans overnight in water and cover. Drain, cover with 300 ml (10 ½ fl oz) fresh water and bring to the boil.

Add one teaspoon of salt and simmer for about 50-60 minutes, until beans are tender.

Preparation time: 8–10 minutes

Cooking time: 30–35 minutes
(or 1 hour 40 minutes if using dried, soaked beans)

Serves: 4

Directions

1. Heat the ghee/oil in a saucepan and sauté the onions, garlic and ginger for approximately ten minutes until the onions are golden brown.

2. Add the ground coriander, cumin, salt, lemon juice, turmeric, and the tomatoes and cook for another five minutes.

3. Add the beans and their cooking liquid; if prepared from dried beans, simmer uncovered until the beans are soft. Add the garam masala and cook for a further minute. Then turn off the heat and garnish with fresh coriander if desired.

Potato & Cauliflower Curry (Aloo Gobi)

450 g (1 lb) cauliflower
200 g (7 oz) potatoes, peeled
1-2 tbsp oil
1 medium onion, finely sliced
1 ½ tsp ginger, finely grated
1 ½ tsp fresh garlic,
finely grated
1 fresh tomato, diced
100 g (3 ½ oz) tinned tomatoes
1-2 fresh green chillies, chopped
1 tsp salt
½ tsp turmeric
½ tsp garam masala
fresh coriander to garnish

Preparation time: 10–15 minutes
Cooking time: 30–40 minutes
Serves: 4

Directions

1. Wash the cauliflower and potatoes, cut them into small pieces and leave to one side.
2. Heat the oil in a pan. Sauté the onions until golden brown. Add the ginger and garlic and stir-fry for 2-3 minutes.
3. Add the fresh and tinned tomatoes, chillies, salt and turmeric and cook for a further 1-2 minutes.
4. Add the cauliflower florets and the potatoes, cover the pan and cook for 15-20 minutes until tender, stirring every few minutes.
5. Add the garam masala and cook for a further minute. Garnish with coriander.

58

Mushroom, Peppers, Tomatoes & Onion Curry

2 tbsp ghee/oil
1 tsp white cumin seeds
1 tsp black mustard seeds
1 fresh green chilli, chopped
1 tsp garlic, finely grated
1 tsp ginger, finely grated
1 medium onion, sliced
200 g (7 oz) mushrooms, sliced
3 fresh tomatoes, sliced
1 red pepper, sliced
1 yellow pepper, sliced
$\frac{1}{2}$ tsp turmeric
$\frac{1}{2}$-1 tsp salt
1 tsp garam masala
1 tbsp of lemon juice
fresh coriander to garnish

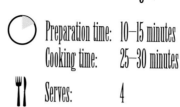

Preparation time: 10–15 minutes
Cooking time: 25–30 minutes

Serves: 4

Directions

1. Heat the ghee/oil in a large frying pan. Grind the cumin seeds and mustard seeds in a pestle and mortar and stir-fry for 30 seconds.

2. Add the green chilli, garlic, ginger and onion and cook until the onions are golden brown.

3. Place the mushrooms, tomatoes, peppers, turmeric and salt in the pan and cook for 5-10 minutes, or until soft.

4. Add the garam masala and lemon juice and cook for a further three minutes.

5. Garnish with coriander and serve.

Potatoes In Gravy Curry

400 g (14 oz) potatoes
2 tbsp ghee/oil
1 tsp cumin seeds
1 tsp black mustard seeds
1 small onion, finely chopped
1 tsp garlic, finely grated
1 tsp ginger, finely grated
1 tsp tomato purée
½ tsp turmeric
1 fresh green chilli, de-seeded
if preferred, and chopped
1 tsp salt
300 ml (10 ½ fl oz) water
1 tsp garam masala
1 tbsp lemon juice
fresh coriander to garnish

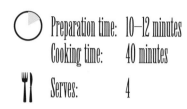

Preparation time: 10–12 minutes
Cooking time: 40 minutes

Serves: 4

Note

You can use boiled potatoes in
this dish to save cooking time.

Directions

1. Peel and cut the potatoes into small pieces.

2. Heat the ghee/oil. Grind the cumin and mustard seed
   in a pestle and mortar and stir-fry for one minute.

3. Add the onion and sauté until golden brown,
   then add the garlic and ginger and stir-fry for
   1-2 minutes.

4. Add the tomato purée, turmeric, chilli and salt, then
   stir and cook for 2-3 minutes.

5. Stir in the potatoes and cook for five minutes. Add
   the water and cook for 10-15 minutes on a medium
   heat. Add the garam masala and lemon juice and
   cook for a further two minutes.

6. Check the potatoes are tender. If not, add some
   more water, leave the lid off the pan and cook for a
   further 5-10 minutes.

7. Garnish with fresh coriander.

63

Tomato Curry

400 g (14 oz) tinned tomatoes
1 tsp salt
2 tsp chilli powder
1 tsp ground coriander
3 tbsp oil
1 tsp white cumin seeds
/₂ tsp black mustard seeds
1 tsp ground fenugreek
1 tsp garlic, finely grated
1 tsp ginger, finely grated
200 ml (7 fl oz) coconut milk
2 tbsp lemon juice
paneer or 1 tbsp double
cream, to garnish

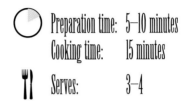

Preparation time: 5–10 minutes
Cooking time: 15 minutes

Serves: 3–4

Directions

1. Place the tinned tomatoes in a large mixing bowl. Add the salt, one teaspoon of the chilli powder and the ground coriander and mix together.

2. Heat the oil in a saucepan. Grind the cumin and mustard seeds in a pestle and mortar. Add these, the fenugreek and the remaining chilli powder and stir-fry for 30 seconds.

3. Add the garlic and ginger and cook for a minute on a moderate heat. Remove from the heat and add the tomato mixture. Return to a medium heat and cook the mixture for 3-4 minutes.

4. Add the coconut milk and reduce the heat. Simmer with the lid on for 4-5 minutes, stirring occasionally. Check and adjust the seasoning to taste.

5. Add the lemon juice to the pan and garnish with cream or paneer pieces. Serve with rice or naan bread.

Potato & Aubergine Curry (Aloo Bhutoun)

450 g (1 lb) small aubergines

1 ½ tsp salt

1 tsp mango powder

1 tsp garam masala

1 tbsp oil

1 medium onion, finely sliced

1 ½ tsp ginger, finely grated

1 ½ tsp of fresh garlic,
finely grated

1 fresh tomato, diced

150 g (5 oz) tinned tomatoes

1-2 fresh green chillies,
chopped

½ tsp turmeric

400 g (14 oz) potatoes,
peeled and diced

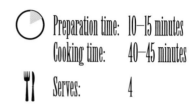

Preparation time: 10–15 minutes

Cooking time: 40–45 minutes

Serves: 4

Note

If small aubergines are
unavailable then you can
use large aubergines

Directions

1. Wash the small aubergines and slit into quarters –
   do not cut all the way through.

2. Mix together half to one teaspoon of the salt, the
   mango powder and the garam masala. Stuff the
   small aubergines with this mixture.

3. Heat the oil in a pan. Sauté the onion until golden
   brown. Add the ginger and garlic and stir-fry for
   2-3 minutes. Add the fresh and tinned tomatoes, the
   remaining salt, the chillies and the turmeric and
   cook for a further 3-4 minutes.

4. Add the potatoes, stir well and cook for five minutes.
   Add the aubergines and cook for 15-20 minutes until
   the potatoes are tender.

Blackeye Bean Curry

400 g (14 oz) blackeye beans
300 ml (10 ½ fl oz) water
1 ½ tsp salt
2 tbsp ghee/oil
1 small onion, finely chopped
1 tsp garlic, finely grated
1 ½ tsp ginger, finely grated
1 tsp ground coriander
1 tsp ground cumin
2 tbsp lemon juice
½ tsp turmeric
150 g (5 oz) tinned tomatoes
½ tsp garam masala
fresh coriander

Note

You can use tinned
blackeye beans. Drain
and rinse them and follow
the recipe from step 2.

Preparation time: Soak beans overnight, plus
8–10 minutes

Cooking time: 1 hour 30 minutes
or using tinned beans 30–35 minutes

Serves: 6

Directions

1. Soak the beans overnight, covered. Drain, cover
   with the water and bring to the boil. Add a teaspoon
   of the salt and simmer for about 45 minutes, until
   beans are tender.

2. Heat the ghee/oil in a saucepan and sauté
   the onions, garlic and ginger for approximately
   5-10 minutes until the onions are golden brown.

3. Add the remaining salt, the ground coriander,
   cumin, lemon juice, turmeric and tomatoes and cook
   for another five minutes. Add the beans and their
   cooking liquid.

4. Simmer, uncovered, until the beans are soft. Add
   the garam masala and garnish with fresh coriander.

69

White Chickpea Curry (Chitai Sholay)

400 g (14 oz) white chickpeas
(tinned chickpeas can
be used)

425 ml (15 fl oz) water

2 tsp salt

2 tbsp ghee/oil

1 black cardamom
or 3 green cardamom

1 tsp coriander seeds

1 cinnamon stick

1 medium onion, finely chopped

1 tsp garlic, finely grated
or chopped

1 tsp ginger, finely grated
or chopped

150 g (5 oz) tinned tomatoes

1 tsp chilli powder

1 tsp chana masala

1 tbsp lemon juice

1 tsp garam masala

Note

You can make black (kala)
chickpea curry in the same
way by substituting black
chickpeas in place of
white chickpeas.

Preparation time: Soak dry beans overnight, plus
10–12 minutes

Cooking time: 1 hour 40 minutes
or using tinned chickpeas 30–40 minutes

Serves: 4

Directions

1. Wash and soak the white chickpeas in a generous
   amount of water overnight. Drain and place with the
   water and one teaspoon of the salt in a saucepan and
   boil until the chickpeas are soft. If using dry chickpeas
   boil for 50 minutes-1 hour until the chickpeas are tender.

2. Heat the ghee/oil in a saucepan. Grind the cardamom,
   coriander seeds and cinnamon stick in a pestle and
   mortar or electric grinder. Stir-fry for 10 seconds.

3. Add the chopped onion and sauté until golden brown.
   Then add the garlic and ginger and cook for 2-3 minutes.

4. Add the tinned tomatoes, chilli powder and
   remaining salt and cook for 3-4 minutes. Add the
   chickpeas, water, and the chana masala. Gently stir
   together and cook for 20-30 minutes. Drizzle with
   lemon juice then add the garam masala. (If using
   tinned chickpeas you only need to cook for 10-12
   minutes and begin at step 2.)

5. Serve with plain boiled rice or pooris (page 90).

71

Spinach & Chickpea Lentils (Saag & Chana Dahl)

225 g (8 oz) dried chickpea lentils (Chana Daal)

850 ml (30 fl oz) water

2-3 tbsp ghee/oil

1 tsp white cumin seeds

1 tsp black mustard seeds

1 medium onion, chopped

1 tsp garlic, finely grated

1 tsp ginger, finely grated

1 tsp salt

1 fresh green chilli, chopped

400 g (14 oz) tinned, frozen or trimmed, washed, fresh spinach

½ tsp garam masala

2 tbsp lemon juice

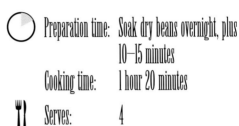

Preparation time: Soak dry beans overnight, plus 10–15 minutes

Cooking time: 1 hour 20 minutes

Serves: 4

Directions

1. Wash and soak the chickpea lentils overnight in a generous amount of water. Drain, then place in a pan with the water, cover, and boil for 30-40 minutes. Strain the chickpea lentils and leave aside.

2. Heat the ghee/oil in a saucepan. Grind the cumin and mustard seeds in a pestle and mortar or electric mixer. Stir-fry for 30 seconds. Add the onion and sauté until golden brown. Add the garlic, ginger, salt and green chilli. Reduce the heat and stir-fry for 4-5 minutes.

3. Add the spinach and mix well. Cook for 20-25 minutes. Add the cooked lentils and stir together. Cook for a further 10-20 minutes and add the garam masala.

4. To finish, drizzle lemon juice over the dish.

73

Yellow Lentil Soup (Moong Daal)

225 g (8 oz) yellow lentils (Moong)

1.2 litres (2 pts) water

1 tsp salt

½ tsp turmeric

2 tbsp ghee/oil

1 medium onion, finely chopped

1 tsp garlic, finely grated

1 fresh green chilli, chopped

1 tsp ginger, finely grated

½ bunch fresh coriander, chopped

½ tsp garam masala

Preparation time: 8–10 minutes

Cooking time: 30–35 minutes

Serves: 4

Directions

1. Wash, drain and place the lentils in a saucepan with the water and boil on a medium heat. Once boiling, add the salt and turmeric and then reduce the heat and simmer for 20 minutes.

2. In a separate pan, heat the ghee/oil. Add the onions, garlic, chillies and ginger and sauté the onions until they are golden brown. Stir occasionally to prevent sticking.

3. Add the onion mixture and the fresh coriander to the lentils in the pan. Stir together, then add the garam masala and continue cooking on a low heat for 1-2 minutes.

4. Transfer to a serving bowl and garnish with more fresh coriander. Serve with rice or naan (page 89).

Dry Lentils (Urid Dahl)

225 g (8 oz) urid lentils
1.2 litres (2 pts) water
1 tsp salt
½ tsp turmeric
2 tbsp ghee/oil
1 medium onion, chopped
1 tsp garlic, finely grated
1 tsp ginger, finely grated
1 fresh green chilli, chopped
1 tbsp lemon juice
1 tsp garam masala

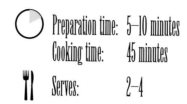

Preparation time: 5–10 minutes
Cooking time: 45 minutes
Serves: 2–4

Directions

1. Wash and rinse the lentils. Place in a saucepan with the water and bring to the boil. Add the salt and turmeric. Simmer for half an hour until the lentils are tender. Check the lentils are tender by rubbing them between your finger and thumb. Be careful not to overcook the lentils as they will split if they are overcooked. Strain and leave aside. Save the stock from the lentils for use later.

2. In a separate pan heat the ghee/oil. Add the onions, garlic, ginger and fresh chillies. Sauté until the onions are golden brown.

3. Add the drained cooked lentils to the onion mixture and stir. Add two tablespoons of the lentil stock and mix well. Cook on a medium to low heat until the water has evaporated, then add the lemon juice and garam masala.

77

Plain Boiled Rice

1 tsp white cumin seeds
(optional)
225 g (8 oz) basmati rice
425 ml (15 fl oz) water
½ tsp salt

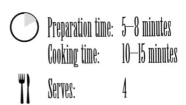

Preparation time: 5–8 minutes
Cooking time: 10–15 minutes

Serves: 4

Directions

1. Grind the cumin seeds in a pestle and mortar then dry-fry in a pan for 30 seconds.

2. Wash and drain the rice. Place in a saucepan on a medium heat with the water, salt and cumin seeds. Bring to the boil and simmer for 10-15 minutes until the rice is tender. Drain and serve.

79

Pilau Rice

Pinch of saffron strands
2 tbsp hot water
225 g (8 oz) basmati rice
2 tbsp ghee/oil/butter
1 shallot or small onion, sliced
3 green cardamom pods
1 cinnamon stick
425 ml (15 fl oz) water
1/2-1 tsp salt

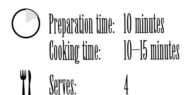

Preparation time: 10 minutes
Cooking time: 10–15 minutes
Serves: 4

Directions

1. Grind the saffron in a pestle and mortar, then place in a small bowl with the hot water and set aside for 5-10 minutes. Then remove the saffron strands.

2. Rinse and drain the rice twice in a sieve.

3. Melt the ghee/oil/butter in a saucepan and sauté the shallot for two minutes. Add the cardamom pods, cinnamon and rice and mix well.

4. Add the water, the saffron mixture and the salt. Bring to the boil on a medium heat then reduce the heat, cover the pan and simmer for 10-15 minutes until the rice has absorbed all the water. Remove the cinnamon stick before serving.

breads, pulses & grains

81

Onion & Peas Rice

1-2 tsp ghee/oil/butter
1 small onion, finely sliced
150 g (5 oz) frozen peas
½ tsp salt
2 curry leaves
½ tsp cumin seeds
225 g (8 oz) basmati rice
425 ml (15 fl oz) water

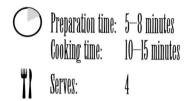

Preparation time: 5–8 minutes
Cooking time: 10–15 minutes

Serves: 4

Directions

1. Melt the ghee/oil/butter in a saucepan and sauté the onion for two minutes.
2. Add the peas, salt, curry leaves, cumin seeds, rice and water, stir and bring to the boil on a medium heat.
3. Reduce the heat, cover the pan and simmer for 10-15 minutes, stirring occasionally, until the rice has absorbed the water. The rice should be soft and tender.

Mushroom Fried Rice

225 g (8 oz) basmati rice
425 ml (15 fl oz) water
2 tbsp oil
1 tsp white cumin seeds
3 curry leaves
250 g (9 oz) mushrooms, chopped
pinch of salt
½ tsp of turmeric

Preparation time: 5–8 minutes
Cooking time: 10–15 minutes

Serves: 4

Directions

1. Rinse the rice and boil in the water until cooked. Set aside to cool.
2. Heat the oil in a pan and stir fry the cumin seeds and curry leaves for 30 seconds. Add the mushrooms, salt, turmeric and the cooked rice and stir until well combined for five minutes. Serve.

Garlic Fried Rice

225 g (8 oz) basmati rice
425 ml (15 fl oz) water
2 tbsp oil
4 garlic cloves, chopped
2 curry leaves
1 tsp salt

Preparation time: 5–8 minutes
Cooking time: 10–15 minutes

Serves: 4

Directions

1. Rinse the rice and then boil in a large pan of water until cooked. Set aside to cool.

2. Heat the oil in a saucepan. Add the garlic and stir-fry until light golden brown. Add the curry leaves and cook for 30 seconds. Add the cooked rice and the salt and cook for a further 3-4 minutes.

3. Serve immediately.

Naan Bread

1 tsp sugar
1 tsp fresh yeast
150 ml (5 fl oz) warm water
200 g (7 oz) plain flour
50 g (2 oz) ghee/oil
1 tsp salt
1 tbsp butter for grilling
1 tsp poppy seeds

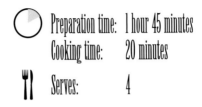

Preparation time: 1 hour 45 minutes
Cooking time: 20 minutes
Serves: 4

Directions

1. Place the sugar and the yeast in a small bowl with the warm water. Mix together until the yeast has dissolved. Leave aside for 10 minutes until the mixture is frothy.

2. Place the flour in a large mixing bowl. Make a well in the middle of the flour and gradually add the ghee/oil, salt and yeast mixture. Mix together using your hands or place in a food processor to form a soft dough. Add a little more water if the dough is too dry.

3. Place the dough on a floured surface and knead for 5 minutes until smooth. Return to the bowl, cover and leave to rise in a warm place for 1 ½ hours (until it has doubled in size).

4. Turn the dough out on a floured surface and knead for 2-3 minutes. Divide into small balls and roll out to a circle of 12 cm (5 in.) diameter and 1 cm (½ in.) thick. Brush each side with butter and place onto a greased sheet of foil. Cook under a very hot grill for 5-10 minutes. Turn twice.

5. Once cooked, sprinkle with poppy seeds and serve straight away, or keep wrapped in foil for later use.

89

Pooris

225 g (8 oz) chapati flour
½ tsp salt
150 ml (5 fl oz) water
600 ml (21 fl oz) oil
75 g (2 ½ oz) chapati flour
for rolling

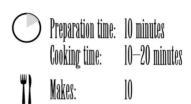

Preparation time: 10 minutes
Cooking time: 10–20 minutes

Makes: 10

Directions

1. Mix the flour and salt together in a bowl. Make a
   well in the centre of the flour. Gradually pour in the
   water and mix together to form a soft dough,
   adding more water if necessary. Knead until smooth
   and leave aside in a warm place for 15 minutes, then
   divide into 10 small balls.

2. Heat the oil in a deep frying pan on a high heat.
   Once hot, turn down to a medium heat.

3. On a lightly floured surface roll out the balls to form
   a thin circular shape of 10-12 cm (4-5 in.) diameter.

4. Deep-fry in batches for 30 seconds to one minute
   on each side until golden brown (pooris do not need
   to be cooked for long if the oil is hot). The pooris
   should puff up. Remove from the pan and drain on
   kitchen towel. Serve immediately or wrap in foil to
   be reheated later.

Chapati/Roti

225 g (8 oz) wholemeal chapati (ata) flour

200 ml (7 fl oz) water

75 g (2 ½ oz) chapati flour for rolling

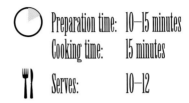

Preparation time: 10–15 minutes
Cooking time: 15 minutes

Serves: 10–12

Directions

1. Place the flour in a large mixing bowl. Make a well in the centre and gradually pour in the water, mixing with your hands, to form a soft dough.

2. Knead for 6-8 minutes, leave aside for 10 minutes and then divide into 10-12 small balls.

3. Roll out the balls on a floured surface to a circle of 12-15 cm (5-6 in.). Shake off any excess flour before cooking.

4. Place a heavy-based frying pan on a high heat. Once the pan is hot, reduce the heat to a medium setting.

5. Place the chapati/roti one by one in the dry pan and cook for 15-20 seconds until it starts to brown slightly and bubble, then turn over. Press down on the chapati with a clean tea towel to cook it evenly for 1-2 minutes, then turn it over and cook the other side for a further 1-2 minutes, until light brown.

93

Gram Flour Bread

100 g (3 ½ oz) chapati (ata) flour

75 g (3 oz) gram flour

½ tsp salt

1 small onion, finely chopped

½ bunch of fresh coriander, chopped

2 fresh green chillies, chopped and de-seeded if preferred

150 ml (5 fl oz) water

2 tsp ghee/oil

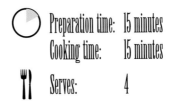

Preparation time: 15 minutes

Cooking time: 15 minutes

Serves: 4

Directions

1. Mix together the chapati flour, gram flour and salt in a large mixing bowl.

2. Add the onion, fresh coriander and chillies to the flour mixture and mix together.

3. Make a well in the flour and gradually add the water and mix to form a soft dough. Cover the dough with a damp tea towel and leave aside for 15 minutes.

4. Knead the dough for 6-8 minutes and divide into 6-8 equal portions. Roll out the portions on a floured surface to a circle of approximately 15-17 cm (6-7 in.).

5. Heat a heavy-based frying pan on a high heat. Once hot, reduce the heat to medium. Individually cook each portion, turning over 2-3 times while cooking. Cook each side briefly for 30 seconds, brushing each side with ghee/oil as you turn over. Cook until light brown.

94

Plain Fried Layered Bread (Parantha)

225 g (8 oz) chapati (ata) flour
½ tsp salt
200 ml (7 fl oz) water
50 g (2 oz) butter
(divided equally per parantha,
see step 2)
2 tbsp ghee/oil

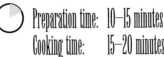

Preparation time: 10–15 minutes
Cooking time: 15–20 minutes

Serves: 6–8

Directions

1. Place the flour in a mixing bowl. Make a well in the flour, add the salt, then, gradually add the water and mix to form a smooth dough. Leave aside for 5-10 minutes, then divide into 6-8 small ball shapes.

2. Roll out each portion to a circle approximately 10 cm (4 in.), then divide the butter and place a knob in the middle of each portion.

3. Fold the left, right, top and bottom sides inwards to encase the butter, creating a square shape. Roll these out again to approximately 12 cm (5 in.) square.

4. Heat a heavy-based frying pan on a high heat then, once hot, reduce the heat to medium. Cook the parantha in turn, cooking each side briefly for 30 seconds to a minute. Then brush with ghee/oil and cook for a further 2-3 minutes. Both sides should be light brown before serving.
   Serve with yoghurt.

97

Potato-stuffed Parantha

Preparation time: 15–20 minutes
Cooking time: 15–20 minutes

Serves: 6–8

225 g (8 oz) chapati (ata) flour

200 ml (7 fl oz) water

4 medium potatoes

1 tsp white cumin seeds

½ bunch of coriander, chopped

1 small onion, finely chopped

1 tbsp lemon juice

1 tsp salt

½ tsp garam masala

1 fresh green chilli, chopped and de-seeded if preferred

2 tbsp ghee/oil

Directions

1. Place the flour in a mixing bowl. Make a well, gradually add the water and mix to form a smooth dough, adding more water if necessary. Leave aside for 5-10 minutes.

2. Wash, peel and boil the potatoes in a saucepan until they are soft. Grind the cumin seeds in a pestle and mortar then dry-fry for 30 seconds in a frying pan.

3. Mash the potatoes and place in a mixing bowl. Add the fresh coriander, onions, cumin seeds, lemon juice, salt, garam masala and fresh chilli to the potatoes and combine together.

4. Divide the flour dough into small ball shapes. Roll out on a lightly floured surface to form thin circles of 10 cm (4 in.) in diameter and spoon 2-3 tablespoons of the potato mixture in the middle of each circle.

5. Wrap the dough around the potato mixture to form a stuffed ball. Roll out the dough to a circle of 12-15 cm (5-6 in.).

6. Heat a heavy-based frying pan on a high heat, reducing to medium once the pan is hot. Cook each side briefly for 30 seconds to a minute, then brush each side with ghee/oil and cook for a further 2-3 minutes until light brown. Serve with yoghurt.

Samosas

FILLING

2 tbsp ghee/butter

400 g (14 oz) potatoes, finely chopped

1 tsp salt

1 tsp white cumin seeds

150 g (5 oz) cooked peas

1 tsp chilli powder

1 tsp mango powder

2 tbsp lemon juice or juice of 1 fresh lemon

1 tsp garam masala

½ bunch of fresh coriander, chopped

Note

You can make meat samosas in the same way. Use lamb mince (Keema recipe-see page 22) instead of the potato mixture as a filling.

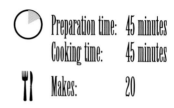

Preparation time: 45 minutes

Cooking time: 45 minutes

Makes: 20

For the filling

1. Heat the ghee/oil in a pan over a medium heat. Cook the potatoes (seasoning with the salt) on a medium heat for 10 minutes, stirring every few minutes.

2. Grind the cumin seeds in a pestle and mortar then, dry-fry for 30 seconds to a minute in a separate small frying pan.

3. Add the cooked peas, chilli powder, mango powder, cumin seeds, lemon juice and garam masala to the potatoes, mix and set aside. Taste the mixture and adjust the seasoning as required. Allow to cool. Add the fresh coriander to the filling and mix.

PASTRY

225 g (8 oz) plain flour
½ tsp salt
75 ml (2 ½ fl oz) warm water

PASTE

25 g (1 oz) plain flour
75 ml (2 ½ fl oz) water

850 ml (30 fl oz) oil for frying

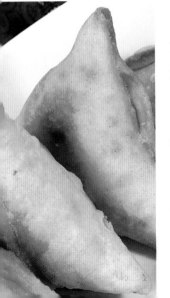

For the pastry

1. Place the flour and salt in a mixing bowl. Make a well in the centre of the flour and gradually pour in the warm water to form a smooth dough.

2. Knead the dough for 3-5 minutes until it is smooth. If the dough is sticky add a little more flour. Cover and leave for 5-10 minutes.

3. Make 8-10 small balls from the dough. Roll out each ball on a lightly floured surface to form a thin round circle shape 12-15 cm (5-6 in.) in diameter. Cook each circle for a few seconds on each side on a medium heat in a heavy-based frying pan. Cut the pastry circle in half and leave covered under a clean tea towel.

To cook

1. Mix together the ingredients for the paste in a small bowl.

2. Shape the pastry halves into cone shapes. Fill the cones with a few tablespoons of the potato mixture. Dampen the top and bottom/side edges of the cones with the paste and pinch together to seal. Leave the filled samosas aside.

3. Fill a deep pan or karahi with the oil and heat on a high heat. Once hot, reduce the heat to medium. Carefully lower the samosas into the oil in small batches. Fry for 2-3 minutes until golden brown, turning over occasionally.

4. Remove from the oil and drain on kitchen towel.

Onion Bhaji

2 medium onions, finely sliced
1 tbsp gram flour
1 tsp mango powder
1/2-1 tsp chilli powder
1/2-1 tsp salt
2 tsp chaat masala
600 ml (21 fl oz) vegetable or sunflower oil

Preparation time: 5–10 minutes
Cooking time: 10–15 minutes

Serves: 3–4

Note

You can substitute the onions with 250 g (9 oz) chopped mushrooms/potatoes or any other vegetables for variation. You can also adjust the seasonings according to taste.

Directions

1. Place all the ingredients, apart from the oil, in a mixing bowl. Mix together with your hands and form small balls with the mixture.

2. Pour the oil into a wok and heat on a high heat. Once hot reduce the heat to medium. The oil should be hot enough that a small piece of the mixture should sizzle.

3. Use a metal, slotted spoon to place the balls into the hot oil and deep fry in batches for 2-3 minutes or until golden brown, turning over while cooking. Remove from the oil and drain on kitchen towel.

Aloo Chana Chaat

1 tsp white cumin seeds

400 g (14 oz) potatoes, peeled, boiled and diced

400 g (14 oz) chickpeas, tinned

1 small onion, finely chopped

½ tsp chilli powder

1 tsp chaat masala

salt to taste

2 tbsp fresh coriander leaves, chopped

2 green chillies, de-seeded, finely chopped

juice of 1 to 1 ½ lemons or 3-4 tbsp lemon juice

3-4 tbsp yoghurt

3-4 tbsp tamarind chutney (optional)

fresh coriander for garnish

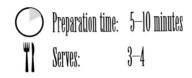

Preparation time: 5–10 minutes

Serves: 3–4

Directions

1. Dry fry the white cumin seeds in a frying pan.

2. In a mixing bowl, carefully combine all the ingredients, except the yoghurt and tamarind chutney and mix well. Taste and adjust the chilli powder, salt and lemon juice to get a tangy and spicy taste.

3. Place on a serving plate and drizzle the yoghurt, then the tamarind chutney (page 112) on top. Garnish with fresh chopped coriander. This can be served as a starter to a main meal.

Aloo Tikka

500 g (18 oz) potatoes, boiled, peeled and mashed

1 tsp cumin powder

1 tbsp cornflour

½-1 tsp chilli powder

½ bunch fresh coriander

½-1 tsp salt to taste

juice of ½ a lemon

1 fresh green chilli, chopped (optional)

1 tsp garam masala

6-7 tbsp vegetable/sunflower oil for frying

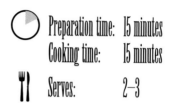

Preparation time: 15 minutes

Cooking time: 15 minutes

Serves: 2–3

Directions

1. Mix all the ingredients together in a mixing bowl, except the oil.

2. Divide into six equal portions and roll them into balls. Flatten each ball between the palms into patties.

3. Heat the oil in a frying pan and shallow fry the patties over a medium heat until golden brown and crisp on both sides. Drain and pat dry on a kitchen towel. Serve hot with a side salad and tamarind chutney (see page 112).

Raita – Onion, Mint & Cucumber

ONION

1 onion, finely chopped
200 ml (7 fl oz) yoghurt
4 tbsp water (optional)
½ tsp salt
2-3 mint leaves to garnish

Directions

Place all the ingredients
except the mint leaves
in a bowl and mix together.
Transfer to a serving
bowl and garnish with
mint leaves.

  Preparation time: 5–10 minutes

Serves: 3–4

CUCUMBER

225 g (8 oz) cucumber
1 medium onion, finely chopped
½ tsp salt
½ tsp fresh mint
200 ml (7 fl oz) yoghurt
4 tbsp water (optional)
fresh mint leaves or a slice of
cucumber to garnish

Directions

Wash, peel and grate the
cucumber. Place in a mixing
bowl with the onion, salt and
mint. Mix in the yoghurt and
optional water and whip
together with a spoon. Garnish
with mint or cucumber.

MINT

200 ml (7 fl oz) yoghurt
4 tbsp water (optional)
1 small onion, chopped
½ tsp mint sauce
½ tsp salt
fresh mint leaves to garnish

Note

Only add water if the
consistency of the yoghurt
that you are using is too thick.

Directions

1. Place the yoghurt in a bowl
   and add the water gradually.
   Stir together with a spoon to
   form a smooth
   consistency.

2. Add the onion, mint sauce and
   salt. Stir together with a spoon.
   Transfer to a serving bowl and
   garnish with fresh mint leaves.

Mango Chutney

500 g (18 oz) fresh mango
1 small onion, finely chopped
½ bunch coriander, chopped
1 tbsp sugar
½–1 tsp salt
1 tsp chilli powder
1 tsp ginger, finely grated
1 tsp garam masala

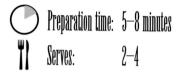

Preparation time: 5–8 minutes
Serves: 2–4

Directions

Wash, peel and dice the mango into small chunks
then place in a blender. Add onion, fresh coriander,
sugar, salt, chilli powder, ginger and garam masala
and blend together for a further minute. Transfer to
a serving bowl.

Tamarind Chutney

2 tbsp tamarind paste
5 tbsp hot water
 tsp chilli powder
½ tsp ground ginger
½ tsp salt
2-3 tsp sugar
fresh coriander to garnish

Preparation time: 5 minutes

Serves: 4–6

Directions

1. Place the tamarind paste in a mixing bowl. Gradually add the hot water and mix together.

2. Add the chilli powder, ginger, salt and sugar to the mixture and stir well. Check seasonings and adjust according to taste.

3. Transfer to a serving dish and garnish with a few sprigs of fresh coriander.

113

Apple Chutney

3-4 spring onions
½ bunch fresh coriander
1 medium cooking apple
1 tsp salt
1 tsp sugar
coriander or apple, to garnish

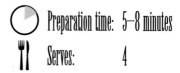

Preparation time: 5–8 minutes
Serves: 4

Directions

1. Wash, dry and finely chop the spring onions and fresh coriander.
2. Wash the cooking apple, peel and chop it into small pieces and place in a blender with the chopped spring onions, coriander, salt and sugar.
3. Blend together for a few seconds until it forms a paste. Transfer to a small bowl and garnish with a few sprigs of fresh coriander or slices of apple.

Ras Gullai

1.7 litres (3 pts) full fat milk

2 tbsp white vinegar

1 tsp fine semolina

225 g (8 oz) sugar

850 ml (30 fl oz) water

6-8 green cardamom pods, crushed

pistachio nuts to garnish

Note

If you would prefer to make the ras gullai sweeter then add extra sugar to taste.

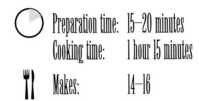

Preparation time: 15–20 minutes

Cooking time: 1 hour 15 minutes

Makes: 14–16

Directions

1. Boil the milk in a saucepan and add the vinegar. When the milk curdles, sieve the milk so you are left with only the curd of a dry consistency.

2. Add the semolina to the curd and knead either by hand or in a food mixer to form a smooth dough. Make about 10-12 small balls from the curd dough, 2 ½ cm (1 in.) diameter.

3. Place the sugar, water and crushed cardamoms in a saucepan and boil for 15-20 minutes until it forms a light syrup. Place the small balls in the syrup. Gently coat the balls in the syrup.

4. Simmer on a low heat for 30-45 minutes, stirring gently. Serve, garnished with pistachio nuts.

Ras Malai

2.7 litres (6 pts) milk
3 tbsp white vinegar
1.2 litres (2 pts) water
180 g (6 ½ oz) sugar
6-8 green cardamom pods, crushed
1 tsp rosewater
pistachio nuts, to garnish

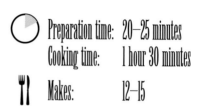

Preparation time: 20–25 minutes
Cooking time: 1 hour 30 minutes

Makes: 12–15

Directions

1. Boil half the milk in a saucepan and add the vinegar. Once the milk curdles sieve the milk so you are left with only the curd of a dry consistency.

2. Knead the curd either by hand or in a food mixer to form a smooth dough. Make 12-15 small patties from the dough.

3. Heat the water, two tablespoons of the sugar and the crushed cardamom pods in a saucepan.

4. Place the patties in the water mixture and simmer for half an hour, then set aside.

5. Boil the remaining milk in a large saucepan then reduce the heat and simmer until the milk has halved in quantity. Add the remaining sugar and stir until dissolved. Cook for 10-15 minutes then add the rosewater.

6. Take the patties out of the water mixture and place in the pan with the milk mixture. Leave for an hour to cool, and serve garnished with pistachio nuts.

Gulab Jaman

600 g (1 lb 6 oz) milk powder
200 g (7 oz) self-raising flour
1 tbsp fine semolina
1 tsp ghee/oil
700 ml (25 fl oz) milk
600 ml (21 fl oz) oil
450 g (1 lb) sugar
1.2 litres (42 fl oz) water
6 green cardamom pods, crushed
pistachio nuts, to garnish

Note

You can adjust the amount of sugar to taste.

Preparation time: 20–25 minutes
Cooking time: 45–50 minutes

Makes: 55–60

Directions

1. Mix the milk powder, flour, semolina and ghee/oil together then gradually add the milk until it forms a smooth dough.

2. Divide the dough into small balls approximately 2 ½ cm (1 in.) wide and set aside.

3. Heat the oil in a large pan or wok on a high heat. Once hot reduce the heat to medium-low. Deep fry the balls in batches until they are golden brown turning them over occasionally so they cook evenly. Remove from the oil with a slotted/perforated metal spoon and place on kitchen towel to remove any excess oil.

4. Place a separate saucepan on a gentle heat and boil the sugar, water and cardamom pods for 15-20 minutes until it forms a light syrup. Remove from the heat.

5. Place the fried balls into the syrup and stir gently. Put the pan back on the heat and simmer for 5-10 minutes then take off the heat. Leave to stand for 10 minutes before serving. Garnish with pistachio nuts.

Sweet Rice With Saffron

1 pinch saffron

2 tbsp hot water

225 g (8 oz) basmati rice

1.2 litres (2 pts) water

225 g (8 oz) sugar

3 tbsp ghee/butter

3 green cardamom pods, crushed

3 cloves

25 g (1 oz) sultanas

handful pistachio nuts

handful flaked almonds

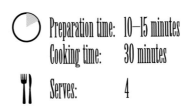

Preparation time: 10–15 minutes

Cooking time: 30 minutes

Serves: 4

Directions

1. Place the saffron in a small bowl with two tablespoons of hot water and leave aside for 5-8 minutes, then remove the saffron strands. The saffron should have coloured the water.

2. Rinse the rice twice and place in a saucepan with one litre (35 fl oz) of the water and the saffron water. Bring to the boil, stirring occasionally. Once the rice is half cooked remove from the heat and strain. Set aside.

3. In a separate saucepan boil the sugar and the remaining 200 ml (7 fl oz) water until the mixture forms a light syrup. Pour over the rice and mix well.

4. Heat the ghee/butter in another saucepan. Place the crushed cardamom pods, cloves, sultanas and pistachio nuts in the pan. Stir together for one minute. Pour the mixture over the rice and stir together. Leave the rice in the pan for 3-4 minutes on a low heat until the rice has absorbed the syrup. Garnish with almond flakes.

Lassi

425 g (15 oz) plain yoghurt
275-425 ml (10-15 fl oz) water
1 tbsp sugar
½ cup crushed ice (optional)
1 tsp cardamom pods (optional)
1-2 tsp pistachio nuts (optional)

Note

Add less or more water
depending on the type of
consistency you like.

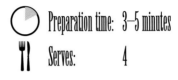

Preparation time: 3–5 minutes

Serves: 4

Directions

1. Place all the ingredients in a blender and blend
   together for a few minutes until frothy.
2. Pour into a tall glass and serve.

Glossary

A

Aloo	Potatoes
Adhrak	Ginger
Ata	Chapati flour

B

Bhutoun	Aubergines
Bindia	Okra
Badam	Almonds
Besan	Gram flour (see)

C

Chite Sholay	white chickpeas

D

Dahi	yoghurt
Daal	lentils
Dalchini	cinnamon sticks
Dhaniya	fresh coriander

G

Garam masala	blend of cumin, black cardamom, coriander seeds, cinnamon and cloves
Ghee	clarified butter
Gram flour	a flour made from ground chickpeas

H

Haldi	turmeric

J

Jeera	cumin seeds

K

Karahi	Heavy-based Indian cooking pan
Korma	mild curry
Kala	black
Kali mirch sabat	black peppercorns

L

Lassi	popular yoghurt-based drink

126

Lachi	cardamom pods
Lasan	garlic

M

Masala	blend of spices
Mutter	peas
Methi	fenugreek

O

Oil	vegetable or olive or sunflower

P

Paneer	Indian cheese
Parantha	fried, layered bread
Pista	pistachio nuts

R

Roti	Indian bread
Rai	mustard seeds

S

Saag	spinach
Sholay	chickpeas

T

Tava	Heavy-based cooking pan for cooking roti/chapati

V

Vindaloo	hot curry

Conclusion

Hopefully you will enjoy trying out this range of recipes. The dishes are authentic and what any family from the Indian sub-continent might eat at home. As well as being tasty, they are easy to prepare and nutritious.

The choice of food from the Indian sub-continent is huge; there are so many different recipes to choose from it would be impossible to include them all in one book.

Many people in Asia follow a vegetarian diet so anybody wanting meat free dishes, can still enjoy spicy food. You will now be able to create some of the most famous and familiar Indian dishes, as well as some lesser known regional classics. They might look rather different from those ordered at a restaurant because there are no additives or artificial colourings used.

Whatever aspect of traditional Indian cuisine you are looking to make, you'll find examples in this book. So, happy cooking, and above all, have fun!